TOP 10 WORST
VOLCANIC ERUPTIONS

Louise and Richard Spilsbury

PowerKiDS press

New York

Published in 2017 by
The Rosen Publishing Group, Inc.
29 East 21st Street, New York, NY 10010

Cataloging-in-Publication Data

Names: Spilsbury, Louise.
Title: Top 10 worst volcanic eruptions / Louise and Richard Spilsbury.
Description: New York : PowerKids Press, 2017. | Series: Nature's ultimate disasters | Includes index.
Identifiers: ISBN 9781499430851 (pbk.) | ISBN 9781499430875 (library bound) | ISBN 9781499430868 (6 pack)
Subjects: LCSH: Volcanoes--Juvenile literature.
Classification: LCC QE521.3 S65 2017 | DDC 551.21--dc23

Produced for Rosen by Calcium
Editors for Calcium Creative Ltd: Sarah Eason and Harriet McGregor
Designers: Paul Myerscough and Simon Borrough
Picture research: Rachel Blount

Picture credits: Cover: Shutterstock: Fotos593 (bottom), Viktoriya (right); Inside: William Rose 13; Shutterstock: Alexey Arkhipov 15, Beboy 4–5, Bikeriderlondon 17, Alfredo Cerra 4, Crobard 21, Ecco3d 19, NoPainNoGain 7, Byelikova Oksana 23, Photovolcanica.com 1, Volker Rauch 25, Wead 6–7; Wikimedia Commons: Jialiang Gao (peace-on-earth.org) 27, U.S. Geological Survey Photograph taken by Richard P. Hoblitt 11, Stephan Schulz 9.

Manufactured in the United States of America
CPSIA Compliance Information: Batch #BW17PK: For Further Information contact Rosen Publishing, New York, New York at 1-800-237-9932.

Contents

VOLCANO DANGER

An erupting volcano is spectacular but danger... Poisonous gas, hot ash, and molten rocks spi... hole or crack in the ground. The hot, liquid rock is called lava. As it flows down the sides of the volcano, it cools to form solid, black rock. An erupting volcano is an **active volcano**.

How Dangerous?

Some active volcanoes erupt gently most of the time. Others only erupt occasionally and they are usually more violent and dangerous. Mount Vesuvius is an active volcano that is likely to erupt in the near future. When it erupted in AD 79, thousands of people in the nearby Roman city of Pompeii died. A **dormant** volcano is one that has not erupted for hundreds or even thousands of years. It is quiet now, but it may erupt again. An **extinct** volcano is the safest type of volcano, because it will never erupt again.

This is the body of a person who was killed during the Vesuvius eruption in AD 79.

Measuring Disaster

Hundreds of small earthquakes are caused as **magma** rises up through cracks in Earth's **crust**.

→ **meters** are used **ct** earthquakes.

Temperatures around the volcano rise as activity increases.

→ **Thermal imaging** techniques and **satellite** cameras can be used to detect heat around a volcano.

When a volcano is close to erupting, it starts to release gases. The higher the sulfur content of these gases, the closer the volcano is to erupting.

→ Gas samples may be taken and **chemical sensors** used to measure sulfur levels.

Natural disasters have taken place since Earth was formed. People have many ways of deciding what the world's worst natural disasters have been, from the deadliest disaster to the costliest. This book includes some of the worst disasters in history.

VOLCANOES IN ACTION

How does red-hot magma from deep inside Earth explode through Earth's surface as a volcano? Volcanoes happen because of the way Earth is made.

Layers of Earth

Earth has three main layers. The **core**, or center, is a ball of solid metal. This is the hottest part of the planet. The **mantle**, above the core, is the widest section of Earth and consists of the partly melted rock we call magma. Magma is very hot: between 1,300 and 2,400 degrees Fahrenheit (700–1,300°C). We live on the crust, a relatively thin layer of solid rock at the surface. The crust is split into large pieces called **tectonic plates**. These plates fit together like a jigsaw puzzle and float on the mantle beneath them. Volcanoes usually form in two types of places. The first is where tectonic plates meet and the second is where the magma beneath Earth's crust is extra hot.

After many eruptions, lava cools, hardens, and builds up around the opening in the crust, forming **cone**-shaped volcanic mountains.

6

How Volcanic Eruptions Happen

When magma comes out of a volcano, it is called lava.

The sides of a volcano are called a cone.

Pressure from the solid rock around the magma forces it up to the surface until magma, gas, and ash explode from an opening called the central vent.

Magma squeezes through gaps in tectonic plates and collects below the crust.

MOUNT ST. HELENS

10

In 1980, the Mount St. Helens volcano among the Cascades Mountains in the state of Washington had been dormant, or asleep, for more than 120 years. Then at 8:32 a.m. on May 18, it erupted in an event that became the worst volcanic disaster ever in North America.

Mount St. Helens

Deafening Disaster

The eruption turned a beautiful mountain covered in forest into a gray, empty wilderness. A total of 57 people and thousands of animals, including deer, elk, and bears, were killed. Clearing up the event cost the country more than one billion dollars.

On the Record

The eruption blew off a 1,307-foot (396 m) section of the north side. It slid down the mountain and covered a huge area of land below.

Volcanic gases exploded from the side of the volcano in a **lateral blast**. This blast traveled at speeds of 670 miles (1,078 km) per hour. It destroyed everything in its path up to about 8 miles (13 km) away.

Mount St. Helens' volcanic cone was totally blasted away by the 1980 eruption.

Between 8 miles (13 km) and about 13 miles (21 km) away, the blast flattened trees as though they were little more than toothpicks.

The eruption caused mudflows, **pyroclastic flows**, and floods. Valleys up to 17 miles (27 km) away were covered in deep mud and **debris**.

The eruption spat out a column of gas and ash 16 miles (26 km) high. Some of this ash blew as far as central Montana. The ash cloaked Spokane, Washington, about 250 miles (400 km) away from the volcano, in total darkness.

9 MOUNT PINATUBO

By the early months of 1991, the Mount Pinatubo volcano on the island of Luzon in the Philippines had been dormant for more than 500 years. But, on June 15, 1991, it exploded in one of the world's most devastating eruptions.

Mount Pinatubo

Evacuation

In 1990, a huge earthquake occurred 62 miles (100 km) northeast of Pinatubo. **Volcanologists** started to study the volcano. By June 12, 1991, as further earthquakes and small explosions continued, they warned the 58,000 people living within 19 miles (30 km) of the volcano to **evacuate**. They escaped just in time.

On the Record

The cloud of ash from Mount Pinatubo turned day into night over central Luzon.

Mount Pinatubo ejected more than 1 cubic mile (4 cu km) of volcanic materials into the air. This created a massive cloud of volcanic ash that rose 22 miles (35 km) high. It grew to more than 300 miles (480 km) across.

Within hours of the eruption, heavy rains began to wash volcanic ash and debris from the slopes onto the surrounding lowlands. This caused giant, fast-moving mudflows. About 300 people still in the area were killed when these flows flattened their houses, and 100,000 people lost their homes.

Almost 20 million tons (18.1 million mt) of sulfuric ash were blasted into the **atmosphere**. The ash spread all around the world in just three weeks. It blocked the sunlight and caused global ground temperatures to fall by 1 degree Fahrenheit (0.5° C) for two years.

8 EL CHICHÓN

In 1982, it had been so long since El Chichón last erupted, in the fourteenth century, that many people thought it was extinct. Then, in March and April, a series of terrible eruptions took place. They became the worst disaster in Mexico's recent history.

El Chichón

Death and Destruction

The eruptions killed more than 1,900 people and devastated over 20,000 homes. The disaster cost Mexico a lot of money because farm cattle and coffee, cocoa, and banana farms were destroyed. The eruption produced a huge cloud of gases that circled the planet for three weeks.

On the Record

On March 28, El Chichón erupted and spewed a huge cloud of gas and ash into the air. It rose 17 miles (27 km) into the atmosphere in less than an hour.

The eruption, which lasted two to three hours, shot out fragments of rock that dropped onto houses like bombs. Volcanic material fell down the sides of the volcano, causing major fires.

The eruptions created a new 0.6-mile-wide (1 km), 984-foot-deep (300 m) **crater** that now contains a shallow lake.

After the first eruption, some people who had left the area returned. But on April 4, 1982, the volcano erupted again. Pyroclastic flows of fast-moving hot gas, ash, and rock traveled up to 5 miles (8 km).

The ash fell to Earth and covered 9,270 square miles (24,000 sq km) of land.

MOUNT VESUVIUS

1

Mount Vesuvius in the Bay of Naples, southern Italy, formed about 200,000 years ago. When it erupted violently and suddenly in AD 79, it buried the nearby cities of Pompeii and Herculaneum. Thick ash from the volcano kept the bodies of the victims hidden until they were dug up 1,600 years later.

Mount Vesuvius

Warning Signs

In AD 62, a large earthquake shook Pompeii. This was then followed by minor quakes, which became worse just before the eruption, as gases built up in the cone. At that time, people did not know about the connection between earthquakes and volcanoes.

14

On the Record

The pressure of gases and magma rising to the surface of Vesuvius pushed out the thick layer of hard lava that plugged the vent at the top of the crater.

The eruption sent a cloud of incredibly hot rock and gas into the sky. It reached a height of 18 miles (30 km). This plunged the surrounding area into darkness.

Vesuvius is the only active volcano in all of mainland Europe.

The ruins of Pompeii include houses, streets, stores, and amphitheaters.

A massive pyroclastic flow raced down the northwest slopes. It buried Herculaneum in almost 70 feet (20 m) of volcanic material. More rivers of rock, gas, and ash flowed through Pompeii, 6 miles (10 km) away.

Victims died when they choked on volcanic ash and gas, were crushed by collapsing buildings, or from the extreme heat produced by the pyroclastic flow.

6 SANTA MARIA

When the 12,400-foot-high (3,772 m) Santa Maria volcano erupted in southwest Guatemala on October 25, 1902, it devastated the surrounding area, which was covered with small farms.

Santa Maria

Darkening Skies

Before October 25, people did not realize that earthquakes in southwest Guatemala were signals that Santa Maria might erupt. When the volcano blew, it killed more than 5,000 people, blackened the skies over Guatemala for days, and destroyed most of the country's important coffee crop for that year.

On the Record

The sound of the volcano exploding was heard as far away as Costa Rica, 530 miles (850 km) south of Santa Maria.

The main eruption lasted for almost 20 hours and shot out a column of ash and gas that reached 16 miles (28 km) into the atmosphere.

Ash from the Santa Maria eruption was found as far away as San Francisco, California.

Santa Maria has been having small eruptions almost constantly since the 1920s.

As well as ash and toxic gas, the eruption threw out lumps of hot and cold **pumice** rock. They rained down on nearby buildings.

The eruption spat out more than 2.5 cubic miles (10 cu km) of material. It covered the land around the volcano up to 16 feet (5 m) deep.

5 NEVADO DEL RUIZ

The Nevado del Ruiz volcano in Colombia, South America, had been dormant for a long time when it began to gently rumble in 1985. Even then, people still believed it was safe until suddenly, on November 13, the volcano burst into life with catastrophic results.

Nevado del Ruiz

Deadly Lahars

Nevado del Ruiz is 17,457 feet (5,321 m) tall, the highest of the Colombian volcanoes. There had been a deadly eruption before, in 1845, when a huge **lahar** traveled more than 40 miles (70 km) downstream and killed over 1,000 people.

On the Record

Nevado del Ruiz threw millions of tons of hot, burning ash into the air. This dropped onto and melted the snow and ice on top of the volcano, causing a mudslide.

Nevado means snow-capped. The top of Nevado del Ruiz volcano is covered in a wide area of snow and ice.

The mudslide was a mixture of mud, ash, and water that was 50 feet (15 m) high in places. It sped down the eastern side of the volcano at 30 miles (50 km) per hour.

Mud also filled a river on the western side of the mountain, causing it to overflow. This created another mudslide that buried 1,000 people in the town of Chinchiná.

The mud buried four towns, including the town of Armero 30 miles (48 km) from the volcano. The town was left under 16 feet (5 m) of mud and 23,000 of its 27,000 inhabitants died.

On the morning of May 8, 1902, Mount Pelée erupted. The volcano, on the island of Martinique, destroyed the city of St. Pierre, killing 30,000 people. This is the largest number of deaths caused by a volcanic eruption in the twentieth century.

Mount Pelée

A Fiery Cloud

Mount Pelée is famous not only for its destructive power but also because its 1902 eruption was the first time people had witnessed and recorded the kind of pyroclastic flow it created. This "fiery cloud" of glowing gas, steam, dust, ash, and pumice rock blasted down its slopes. This type of eruption is now known as "peléan" after Mount Pelée.

On the Record

Animal behavior indicated the first signs of trouble. Yellow ants, centipedes, snakes, and other animals sensed that an eruption was coming. They began to escape down the slopes of the volcano and across nearby fields.

Before the volcano erupted, earthquakes and mudflows had killed several local people. However, there was an important election planned and politicians did not want to delay it by evacuating people.

The sand found on the beach near Mount Pelée is black because it is formed from volcanic rock.

When Pelée erupted, a giant cloud of burning gas sped down its slopes at speeds of more than 100 miles (160 km) per hour into the city of St. Pierre. In minutes, the city was ruined and its inhabitants suffocated and burned to death.

There were only two survivors in St. Pierre. Léon Compère Léandre, a shoemaker, escaped the burning ash in his basement. Auguste Ciparis, a convicted murderer, was protected from the heat and shock by his dungeon's huge stone walls.

3 KRAKATOA

When the volcano of Krakatoa in Southeast Asia erupted on August 26, 1883, the energy it released produced the loudest sound ever reported in history. The noise was so loud that people in Australia, 2,200 miles (3,500 km) away, heard it.

Krakatoa

A Cloud of Ash

There was a series of eruptions that grew more and more violent until Krakatoa jetted out a cloud of ash and pumice rock. The energy released by the volcano was similar to that of 15,000 nuclear bombs!

On the Record

The eruptions of Krakatoa released 5 cubic miles (21 cu km) of rock and sent black clouds of ash up to 50 miles (80 km) high above the ocean.

When the ash fell down to Earth, it covered 300,000 square miles (800,000 sq km) of land. As it fell, it cloaked the area in darkness for more than two days and kept plants from growing for five years.

Krakatoa is still active today. Local people, such as these fishermen, live and work near the volcano despite its ever-present danger.

After the eruption, the volcano collapsed. This caused **tsunamis**, which traveled as far as Hawaii, 6,000 miles (10,000 km) away. The biggest tsunami was 120 feet (37 m) high. The waves battered the coasts of Java and Sumatra, killed 36,000 people, and destroyed 165 coastal villages.

Gases released by Krakatoa hung in the atmosphere, blocking the sun. This caused Earth's average temperature to drop by up to 2.2 degrees Fahrenheit (1.2° C). Earth's temperatures did not return to normal until 1888.

One of the worst eruptions on Earth happened in 1646 BC on Thera, an island today known as Santorini, near Crete in Greece. Experts are not sure whether there was one or more explosions. They do know that the eruption was devastating and killed 20,000 people.

Santorini

A Lost World

The eruptions buried a town on Thera, called Akrotiri, under a thick blanket of ash and pumice. It remained hidden for more than 3,500 years, until workers digging out pumice to make cement found it. No bodies were found in the town, so its inhabitants must have fled in time.

On the Record

The explosion on Thera is thought to have released as much energy as 40 nuclear bombs. It was 100 times more powerful than the eruption at Pompeii in AD 79.

During the eruption, fast-moving pyroclastic flows poured into the sea. As they hit the water, they caused enormous tsunamis that raced across the ocean and hit Crete.

Today, there are still thick layers of white pumice and black ash on the islands that make up Santorini and its neighbors.

The eruption also caused pyroclastic flows of pumice, which can float. They sped across the water until their load of burning hot rock hit land many miles away.

The volcano released up to 14 cubic miles (60 cu km) of magma. Scientists have found volcanic deposits up to 100 feet (30 m) thick at a distance of 19 miles (30 km) from the volcano.

On nearby Crete, thousands of people were killed by the tsunamis and pyroclastic flows.

1 MOUNT TAMBORA

The explosion of Mount Tambora in 1815 is the largest ever recorded. It ranked a seven, or "super-colossal," on the Volcanic Explosivity Index, the second-highest rating in the index. The volcano, which is still active, is on the island of Sumbawa in Indonesia.

Mount Tambora

Deafening Disaster

The 1815 eruption was so loud that soldiers 800 miles (1,280 km) away on the island of Java were sent to fight because their leaders mistook the sound for cannon fire! Around 10,000 islanders were killed immediately, as hot gas and rock sped down the mountain.

On the Record

Mount Tambora ejected around 36 cubic miles (150 cubic km) of ash and rock into the air.

Before it erupted, Mount Tambora was about 14,000 feet (4,300 m) high. Today, it is just 8,930 feet (2,722 m) high.

The eruption of Mount Tambora left a crater 3.7 miles (6 km) across.

Pyroclastic flows raced down the slopes at more than 100 miles (160 km) per hour, all the way to the ocean 25 miles (40 km) away.

The eruption spewed 60 million tons of sulfur into the atmosphere.

While the death toll of people living on Sumbawa and the surrounding coastal areas was very high, even more people died after the eruption as a result of global climate change. These changes turned 1816 into the "year without a summer" for much of Europe, causing terrible famine. It is estimated that, in total, the eruption caused the deaths of almost 100,000 people.

WHERE IN THE WORLD?

Mount Vesuvius

Santorini

This map shows the location of all the volcanic eruptions featured in this book.

Mount Pinatubo

Krakatoa

INDIAN OCEAN

Mount Tambora

The area around the edge of the Pacific Ocean marks the meeting point of different tectonic plates. It is known as the "Ring of Fire." Looking at this map, what evidence can you see to help you explain why the area got this name?

Why do you think it is important to study volcanoes from history? How might learning about the causes and effects of eruptions in the past help save lives and property today?

Read the case studies about Mount Tambora, the number 1 volcano on this map, and Mount St. Helens, the number 10 volcano. How do they differ?

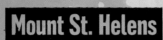
Mount St. Helens

ATLANTIC
OCEAN

El Chichón

Mount Pelée

PACIFIC
OCEAN

Santa Maria

Nevado del Ruiz

Many deaths following a volcanic eruption are not caused directly by the volcano, but by subsequent disasters, such as tsunamis. What examples can you find in this book to support this statement?

GLOSSARY

active A volcano that could erupt at any time.

ash Tiny pieces of burned rock.

atmosphere The blanket of gases that surrounds Earth.

chemical sensors Devices that detect chemicals present.

cone The sides of a volcano.

core The ball of burning-hot metal at the center of Earth.

crater The bowl-shaped hole at the top of a volcano.

crust Earth's outer layer of solid rock.

debris Loose waste material.

dormant A volcano that has not erupted for many years.

evacuate Get away from an area that is dangerous to somewhere that is safe.

extinct A volcano that scientists do not think will erupt again.

lahar A mix of water and pieces of rock that form a mudflow that can be fast-flowing and deadly.

lateral blast A volcanic eruption from the sides of a volcano instead of from the top.

lava Hot, liquid rock (called magma) when it erupts from a volcano.

magma Hot, liquid rock below Earth's surface.

mantle The layer inside Earth between the crust and the core.

molten Melted.

pressure A pushing force.

pumice A very lightweight kind of rock.

pyroclastic flows Super-hot avalanches of gas, ash, and dust. They cover everything in a thick layer of ash.

satellite An object in space that travels around Earth.

seismometers Machines that measure the movement of the ground during a volcano or earthquake.

tectonic plates The giant pieces of rock that fit together like a jigsaw puzzle to form Earth's crust.

thermal imaging A technique that detects heat instead of light to make pictures.

tsunamis Huge waves.

volcanologists Scientists who study volcanoes.

FURTHER READING

Books

Furgang, Kathy. *Everything Volcanoes and Earthquakes* (National Geographic Kids Everything). Washington, DC: National Geographic Children's Books, 2013.

Rusch, Elizabeth. *Eruption!: Volcanoes and the Science of Saving Lives*. Boston: Houghton Mifflin Harcourt, 2013.

Volcanoes (DK findout!). New York, NY: Dorling Kindersley, 2016.

Websites

Due to the changing nature of Internet links, PowerKids Press has developed an online list of websites related to the subject of this book. This site is updated regularly. Please use this link to access the list: **www.powerkidslinks.com/nud/volcanic**

INDEX